"Meg Johnson's new book is a furry pink pillow full of blood and teeth. Slyly brilliant, funny, and scary all at the same time, its effect can only be achieved through a careful attention to craft and unwavering clarity. Her psychological portraits of women and our subsciouses—of our indefatigable rage and imagination—of our struggle for power and independence—had me laughing and gasping at the same time."

JENNIFER L. KNOX, AUTHOR OF *DAYS OF SHAME AND FAILURE*

"At once fierce and fragile, the heroines of Meg Johnson's vignettes invite readers to peer through keyholes and riffle pages. Secrets stain characters' careful lives, lending mystery to lyrical poetic fragments. In precise, musical language, Johnson invites us to study the stories behind quotidian thoughts and feelings. *The Crimes of Clara Turlington* reads like a thought police blotter: every nuanced emotion called in and cuffed."

CAROL GUESS, AUTHOR OF *DARLING ENDANGERED*

"Meg Johnson's girl gang teaches you how to make yourself unavailable, even when your body remains in the room. These girls know how to get things done. They attract the gaze and pin it to the ugly consequences of its greed. They're so visible as to be invisible. They laugh until we get the joke. They need naps and dirt naps. They make an uneasy alliance with other creatures who can anticipate a blow—horses, small children, some of us—and when they're lucky, feint."

DANIELLE PAFUNDA, AUTHOR OF *NATURAL HISTORY RAPE MUSEUM*

for my friends

ABOUT THE AUTHOR

Meg Johnson is the author of the full length poetry
collection Inappropriate Sleepover (The National
Poetry Review Press, 2014). Her poems have appeared
in Hobart, Nashville Review, Painted Bride Quarterly,
Sugar House Review, Verse Daily, and others. Meg
started dancing at a young age and worked professionally
in the performing arts for many years. She is the editor
of Dressing Room Poetry Journal and received her MFA
in creative writing from the NEOMFA Program.
Visit Meg at: *www.megjohnson.org*

Print Edition
ISBN: 978-0-9942837-7-1

Published by Vine Leaves Press 2015
Melbourne, Victoria, Australia

Cover photography from Shutterstock.com
Cover design by Jessica Bell
Interior design by Amie McCracken
Coffee stain image designed by Freepik.com

National Library of Australia Cataloguing-in-Publication entry (pbk)
Creator: Johnson, Meg, author.
Title: The Crimes of Clara Turlington / Meg Johnson.
ISBN: 9780994283771 (paperback)
Subjects: Turlington, Clara—Poetry.
Female offenders—Poetry.
Crime—Poetry.
Dewey Number: A821.4

THE **CRIMES** OF
CLARA TURLINGTON

MEG JOHNSON

Vine Leaves Press
Melbourne, Vic, Australia | Athens, Attica, Greece

TABLE °F CONTENTS

I'M NOT A ROBUST GIRL

who knows how to operate
a chainsaw, cutting firewood
into even pieces, untied
hair blowing in the breeze.

I look like I should
be wearing a pinafore.
I look like I should collect
glass unicorn figurines.
I look like a Victorian
in a medical illustration
for swollen glands.

For someone who spends
so much time blowing
her nose, I get a lot of dates.
My thoughts on polio
are fascinating.

If I could work a chainsaw,
I would hit the throttle,
scare off excessive suitors.

MS. KNOTS

I am in knots. In fact
I'm currently on tour.
You would think
demonstrations
of my freakishness
would be destructive,
but how many people
can so elegantly transition
themselves from a Lark's
Knot to a Clove Hitch?
This is who I am. Try
to look away. Just try.

SLUGGER

I want to take a bat
to a picket fence
and then weep
with the homeowners
over the wreckage.
I could never be
a suspect, cardigan
and pink lips.
I was taught well
before birth: Smoking
a King Edward cigar
and driving a pick-up
truck, my father, age 13.
When I am turned
into a blind fox,
I can wander toward
old loves and say
it's not my fault.

GIRLY BEAR

I thought I had a good idea
coming on, but it was just
a nap. When I woke up,
I looked up a dream
dictionary website
on my iPhone to see what
"dresses" and "playgrounds"
and "parks" and "jewels"
meant. I was still laying down
as I dug into my unconscious.
How lazy am I? It's not my fault,
really. It's the technology.
At least I don't have a car
so I have to walk everywhere.
When I get the pedestrian
walk sign and a car keeps going,
I scowl at the driver, shaming him
as if my walking is saving the world
and his car is a baby killer. I scowl
like a medieval queen who hates
her husband and stands out
in the cold for fun. I scowl like a bear
that ran out of the good honey.
I scowl like an overscheduled,
underpaid woman who wants
to take a nap.

BREAKING UP WITH MARC SUMMERS

Marc Summers' skin is raw
from his fourth shower today.
Marc Summers wants to talk
about our relationship.
About how he feels like he
is dying inside when I eat
cookies in bed or have streaks
of lotion on my legs
I've forgotten to rub in.
That's what he thinks.
That I've forgotten to rub
the lotion in. I pretend
to be drunk when I want
to eat cookies in bed.
He won't fight with me
when he thinks I'm drunk.
If he would look in the recycling
bin, he would know I've only
had orange juice. But he insists
he be ten feet away
from the recycling bin
at all times. It can be sticky.
Like me. Or a human-sized
syrup-drenched waffle.

MUSCLE

I am arm wrestling
an invisible man.
He is invisible
except for his arm.

I want to bite it
like a turkey leg,
but then I would be
disqualified.

The invisible man
might be sexy.
I'd like to find out,
but only after I win.

STER°ID USE

For illness, not ambition,
though it's hard to remember
as the days pass you were actually
prescribed this, the heat generating
off your thighs, your knuckles red
from hitting a punching bag.

You want to write a gentle ode:
The strangers who hit on me when
I had Bell's Palsy will always
have a special place in my heart ...
But you can't concentrate long
enough to finish it.

You imagine yourself throwing
a chair when someone at work
says there'll be extra meetings this year.
What about your own work? The time
you must spend with a medical team
examining your sore eyes?

You look at your reemerging polished
teeth in the mirror, your returning smile,
the jewels of a menace.

CONFESSION

Can I tell my sins to a baby?
Would a butterfly be available?
How about a bag of jellybeans?
Look, I did some bad things
and I want to be good. I just don't see
how some dude in the shadows
can possibly help this situation.
I'm really making an effort here.
I only did confession (did confession?)
once, in fourth grade. I'm really down
with the whole ritual of it
and want to try again.
With a butterfly.

THE PLUMBER DID NOT FIND ANYTHING UNUSUAL IN THE PIPES

The plumber said he did not see anything
unusual in the pipes. The plumber said
he did not find my childhood crush
on Art Garfunkel clogging the pipes,
and he did not find the *Sounds of Silence*
album cover lodged anywhere. The plumber
assured me that the black and white photos
of Simon and Garfunkel on the back of the album cover,
which as a kid I thought were homoerotic and sexy
even though I never used those words,
did not do any damage.

The plumber said he did not see me in the pipes
lost and sobbing on a dark country road
with a fireworks display mocking me, my hot tears
grazing my cheeks like smooth explosives.

The plumber said something about roots. I said
I don't have any roots here.

L

Wild thing, I plan
trips to see you,
but I never buy
the tickets.

Wild thing, I am
actually the wild
one. I mailed
you pink underwear.
Did you get them?

Wild thing, I'll tuck
you in. I'll answer
your phone, but
not the door.

Wild thing, I'll write
your name inside
a cheerleading uniform.
Wear it to meet you
by the railroad tracks.

Strangers will think
I'm a drunk college
girl. But I'm a grown
woman. I'd steal horses
for you.

THE HEROINE

When I was no older than seven, I heard a story about a McDonald's in my town being held up by gunmen planning to rob the place. Maybe it was a Burger King, I'm not sure. They locked some of the patrons in the walk-in closet sized refrigerators. Some people had to get down on the sticky (I'm assuming) floor. During the initial commotion when the men revealed their guns and started escorting the employees and customers to their designated areas of surrender, a teenage employee escaped through the drive-through window, ran to a nearby house or business, and called the cops. People gushed about this girl who saved the day. How smart she was. How brave. How fast. But more than anything people marveled at the fact that she must have had narrow hips to fit through the late 80's/early 90's teeny tiny drive through window. *Her hips must be so narrow*, was the mantra of the victory. Her legacy. I asked the universe in my little girl inner monologue that I grow up to be smart, brave, fast, and have narrow hips. Please, let me have narrow hips. I was already a skinny kid, so my wish to not grow up to be hippy was extra ridiculous. I should have wished to never be held at gunpoint, but that never even crossed my mind.

NUBS GIVES ME F°°TIE PAJAMAS

and tells me kidnapping is for sissies. He is a *human steal artist*. I would nod, but I'm trying to stay still as he braids my hair. I ask Nubs if we can go see the Eiffel Tower. He tells me to stop making dirty jokes and I have no idea what he's talking about. I ask Nubs if I can use the computer for a little while before bed. He doesn't know that I'm plotting his death. That I clear all my browsing history except for the *Yo Gabba Gabba* website. He's so stupid. He actually thinks I think about *Yo Gabba Gabba* for hours at a time. I keep trying to get him to take me somewhere tall like the Statue of Liberty so I can push him out a window when no one is looking. I guess I'll just have to poison him.

THE STAIRCASES

One staircase is fighting
with another staircase.
They threaten to light
each other on fire.
They argue about light
wood vs. dark wood
and talk about numbers.
*Thirty-two people in two
months*, brags one staircase.
*I won't even go into
footsteps.*

CRISP

I want to put all of it
in the oven, singe the edges.
Slightly. Let everyone know
it's all there by the ambiguous
burn scent.

Toast the things I can't say.
I had sex yesterday.
But the most revealing thing
from this week happened
when someone (else)
took the cap off his/her pen
then handed it to me.

BUTTER SAD

When I feel so sad
I want to be an elderly
woman churning butter,
I stir cheese dip
and pretend I'm standing
next to a barn. I call out
to the horses. When one
rolls her eyes at me,
I bring up her failed career
as a race horse. She settles
down, but I won't let it go.
*What was your name
in your racing days? Blaze?
More like Meander.*
She reminds me I'm standing
next to a microwave,
talking to myself.

UNDISCLOSED

Underage with a fake
name and an office job,
a forged birth certificate
and thrift store clothes,
I would creep back
to my cubicle at night,
dream of bakeries
and open fields.

I'LL NEVER USE IT

It's a cheesy joke to make
at a bridal shower.
Please. Make me
a toilet paper mummy.
Not a toilet paper bride.
But I mean it.
I shake
my head at
my disposable beauty.

PARTIAL BIOGRAPHY

1
Central Iowa, 1992
Everyone's name is
Sara(h) Lynn(e).

2
Performers (Professional)
I say "Thanks,
you guys!" like
a well-liked
teenage girl, but
I'm really thinking:
this curling iron
can be used
as a weapon.

3
Self-Inflicted Misery
It brings me strange
comfort. Like a pharmacist
with a foreign accent.

4
I'm a Grown-Up, Really
Some have suggested
that I am the evil twin.
But how can that be?
I smell like flowers!

TALENT

The bulging manila envelope,
I don't have to open it
to know it contains cash,
a handgun wrapped in gauze.
You wrote me
a one word compliment
in black marker
on its swollen belly.

When I saw you
last and protested,
you said it wasn't any different
than kissing someone
and slinking away.
I fiddled with my necklace.
I wasn't listening.

CAST °FF

Queen of the cast–off,
you reign over the only two
people ever seen on the fire
escape. First, the man smoking.
Then, the woman crying.

You reign over forgotten stuffed
animals, swollen ankles, torn dollar
bills, people called stupid Americans.

You are the gentlest parole officer
for the dogs with no faces.

Royal of grease, of alleyway break
ups. Of oblivious children and careless
fathers. Of fake IDs and awkward
voicemails. The lonely people
pretending to look at their phones.

You thought monarchy would be
something different than this broken
block. You thought wrong.

LADIES, CALL NOW

Welcome to the *Yes-these-really-are-your-options Hotline*.

Press **1** if you'd like a tattoo artist wearing a gold chain and swim trunks to make a move on you in a hot tub as he chews on a toothpick ...

Press **2** if you'd like men who write scholarly articles to fight over you, but only after you teach them how to throw punches and supply them with pocket knives ...

Press **3** if you'd like to go on a date with a thirty-something male who suggests you watch a *Twilight* movie together ...

Press **4** if you'd like a hot guy to ask you to clean his fish tank ...

Press **5** if you think Saddam Hussein is an endearing nickname for someone to give their penis ...

Press **6** if you think OCD is sexy and/or like to watch a man cry whenever he accidentally spills something ...

Press **7** to speak with a representative ...

CITY PORTRAIT: AKRON, OHIO

Rain falling on
a pile of trash
concealing
a rapist.

That's offensive?
Sorry. I meant
an *aspiring* rapist.

IN PSEUD°NYM, ILLIN°IS

I have as many sundresses
as there are days of the summer.

It doesn't matter
what I wear or don't
wear. It doesn't matter
that I have a face.

He's always horny after
his men's yoga class.

SASHA GREY AND MEGAN FOX

have similar jobs, right?
The media insists
we act like they're different.

I don't mean to talk shit
about either of them, the allure
of pretty raven-haired women
bending over is obvious.

There is just so much bending
over and boob grabbing
that I'm exhausted
from pretending they make money
for different reasons.

Neither of these broads are reciting
Shakespeare. I'm not complaining.
I've spent many hours hiding
in bathrooms from Shakespeare
professors. I'm just saying
that Fox and Grey have similar
bodies of work and that Shakespeare
professors can be really creepy.

AMERICAN ARTIST

I thought doing a naked Mexican Hat Dance would be great…except I wasn't totally naked because I had a hat … and people were confused about why I didn't have clothes on… *And*, as someone pointed out, I'm actually Czech, so what business do I have doing a Mexican Hat Dance?

Don't they get it? I'm trying to push the boundaries of art. I'm going for the unexpected. I'm trying to recreate *modern society*. Didn't they read the program notes?

Is that what they want? An artless society? Because let me tell you, in Europe, people appreciate the symbolism of a naked Mexican Hat Dance.

I LIKE PENISES

but the idea of having one
grosses me out. An extra limb.
One you can't control. No, no,
no, that has never appealed to me,
the dancer I was, knowing
where each piece of my body
was in space. My clit like a space
heater, like a second heart,
a bright planet I rule.

FIVE CHAPTERS

I signed a contract
that said "the artist"
(me) will not violate
the fire code. (# 9 of 27)

*

The next day I pressed
an unlit match
to my bottom gum.
(It's the sulfur…)

*

It's so easy to
accidentally
go to the men's room.

*

I want to tell her
When I was your age,
I had a Pussycat Dolls CD.

*

Do you think being a nun
makes a nun
feel sexy?

FIRST BORN

I am about to give birth
in an evening gown,
my hair in ringlets
with sparkly barrettes.
My jewelry clangs
as I breathe deeply.
I command a nurse
to fix my smudgy
make-up. *Jesus Christ,*
my fourth husband
says. *You're in denial
about what's about
to happen.* He jokes
that I forgot my feather
boa. I tell him that's
ridiculous. Feather boas
shed and I don't need
feathers stuck to
different parts of my body.
*Women sweat when
they're in labor,*
I hiss. *You're clueless.*

UNSWERVING

I see a wire under
my skin. From the top
of my underwear,
inching up my center,
a painless stem. I worry
I am not real. I worry
the wire should be tucked
inside, not forcing its way
out. I tell myself whether
I am human or machine
is no one's business.

YOUR VULVA NEEDS A SHOUT-OUT

Your vulva is hiring a P.R. firm.
Your vulva has a low profile.

Once, in the 90's, Ross said "vulva"
on *Friends*, but that was a long time ago,
and your vulva never really liked
Ross anyway.

Your vulva is hiring a lawyer.
Think of all the times it was robbed
of proper attribution.

A girl with an upcoming Brazilian:
"I'm getting my vagina waxed!"
No, you are not. Your vagina
is waxing *you*.

"I suffer for nothing!" says your vulva,
pouting.

I'M A BEAST

I am a rapper. I rap
to my porcelain dolls.
I can tell they love
my fierce rhymes
when they don't
move their eyes.
And when they look
white.

I am fake pregnant.
Not to trap a man, but
to entertain myself.
It makes me feel skinny!

I am auditioning
to be a puppet. I like
to pull my own strings.
I wish I was at home
pulling my own strings
right now.

You must sit at least two feet
away from me. If you do not
sit two feet away from me,
I will continue to smell
this sharpie marker until
you feel so uncomfortable
you will shiver
with self-hatred.

FAKING IT

Do you ever feel like faking
your own death just so you don't
have to read your work emails?
My parents would probably help me
hide out if it meant I would move
back to Iowa. *They've really lost it*
people would say with pity
when they saw my parents
getting three dinners to go
from the local barbecue joint.
Trying to feed a ghost.

THE SPEAKER IN THE POEM

The speaker in the poem blows a kiss.

[Poet blows a kiss.]

The speaker in the poem winks.

[Poet winks.]

Wanna know a secret?

The speaker in the poem wears black underwear.

[Poet nods.]

The speaker in the poem is your friend.

[Poet hugs themselves.]

The speaker in the poem controls your mind.

[Poet smiles and waves.]

The speaker in the poem …

[Awkward pause long enough to make the audience wonder if there is something wrong with the poet.]

… is the speaker in the poem.

MARGARET KATHERINE, OH NO

Margaret Katherine moans in a fake Russian accent.
Margaret Katherine drives a stick shift.
[I stand on the sidewalk and kick litter.]

Margaret Katherine sings *Sweet Home Alabama* at Karaoke.
Margaret Katherine never returned the book she borrowed.
[I wrote my name in it.]

Margaret Katherine writes in bubble letters.
Margaret Katherine is half an inch taller than me.
[I stole Margaret Katherine's faux fur coat.]

Margaret Katherine stole four of my boyfriends.
Margaret Katherine is saving for retirement.
[She is my twin sister.]

Margaret Katherine wishes she would have
had "stage parents."
Margaret Katherine appeared on *The Price Is Right*.
[I once sat in a ditch for fourteen hours.]

THE LITTLE MERMAID GETS HER LEGS

Let's be honest. After getting legs, the last thing Ariel would want to do is track down some guy she had seen a couple times. Especially after winning the lawsuit and getting her voice back. After living with six sisters and an overbearing father, she'd haul ass to the nearest hotel, get a room, and lock the deadbolt. She would work up the courage to jump from one double bed to the other. Convinced she was a physical prodigy, she'd drag the front desk clerk up to her room to watch. When the girl wearing a purple bra and mini skirt told him she had something to show him, the front desk guy was expecting something else entirely. *Uhhhh, I should get back*, said the clerk after watching the redhead jump on the beds, laughing and repeating the phrase, *Isn't it amazing?* Eventually, Ariel would lie down to rest, but would find herself discovering masturbation. After all of the bed jumping and orgasming, she'd order room service. She still wanted to read all the books at her local library and a part of her still wanted to find Eric. But not today. She had meat and cable channels.

AMERICAN W°MAN; °R, IF THE THREE °RIGINAL AMERICAN GIRL HER°INES WERE GR°WN-ASS W°MEN IN 2013

1: Kirsten

She wasn't suicidal, but
she didn't mind thinking about death.
When she was a child,
it seemed everyone was dying,
even children her age.
She wasn't ungrateful.
She knew she should
treasure her three healthy sons,
her loyal husband.
There was just always so much
work to do. At the office,
she did her own work
and often stayed late
fixing co-workers' projects.
At home, there were mountains
of socks that needed to be washed.
When she would mix up
the boys' underwear,
putting the Batman boxers
in the wrong dresser, her sons
were greatly offended. Even
as a small girl, chore after chore.
She liked to think of herself
one day nestled in the ground,
unable to awake, unable to work.

2: Samantha

She should have remembered
what her grandmother taught her:
actions speak louder than words.
Maybe then, she wouldn't have married
the wrong man. Twice. Oh, Ms.
Parkington. People often forget
she's a double divorcée. Her girlish
looks and bandage dresses distract
from what didn't go as planned.
She's not just gorgeous, married
friends say to bachelors when trying
to set her up on dates. *She's smart
and talented and does a ton
of charity work.* Sam's best friend,
Nellie, gives it to her straight
over martinis. *The clock is ticking.*

3: Molly

She knew when she was a little girl.
She wanted to cradle Emily Bennett
when Emily was afraid of the war. Kiss
her under her desk. She wanted
to be the perfect military daughter,
her father's love her proudest possession.

She has reconciled with her father
after years of estrangement.
Mr. McIntire wanted to meet
his grandchild. He was kind
to Molly's wife when he finally met her,
years after the rest of the family.

I will always love you, Molly, he said.
Molly knew he was telling the truth.

She also knew he would continue to vote conservative, remain in awe of his motorized tie rack, and refer to his sickly pet puggle as *the lady seducer.*

THE GENIE

The genie tells you he is your friend. The genie comes to your house, comes in through the window. The genie sexes up your wife. He is tired of giving. The sex does nothing for your wife. Now she is filled with regret. She jumps from the fourth floor. When you get home, the genie is devouring the turkey, the Jell-O, the wine.

FUTURE QUEEN °F THE WILIS G°ES HUNTING

She liked the crunch of the white snow.
The androgynous bulk of orange
encapsulating her long frame. In town,
there were double takes and a sense
of foreboding. *You look sixteen*, her father said
on seeing her in new ballet clothes.
She was eleven. Bringing down her first
pheasant felt natural. She could imagine
getting pheasants to fall from the sky
without a gun. She could imagine
herself all in white like the fallen snow.

QUEEN BEE, SIMPERING

The nape of my neck is feeling
overexposed. The nape of my neck asked
for her own country house. I took her camping
and she whined about the marshmallows
being too gooey in the S'mores I made her.
That bitch has hermit tendencies.

MY HERMIT TENDENCIES

1
There is something as bad
as going through a break-up.
It's being invited
to watch someone else's break-up.
I didn't know that's what
I had RSVPed yes for.
I just wanted a free lunch.

2
A friend of a friend
says he has Clamato
and I say I'm sorry
and he looks confused.
Apparently, Clamato
is a flavored beer,
not an STD.
(Clam plus tomato.)
I'd rather drink
Bud Light UStaph.
(UTI plus Staph infection.)

3
While sight-seeing, I witness
a congressman speaking
about atheists at a rally. *They do
have a holiday. It's April First!*
Can I go home now?

MONARCH OF THE FORGOTTEN BLOCK

The neighborhood children didn't know what to think of me.

> Single/Childless/Grown-up/Working woman/Rents a house/Wears a bikini in the backyard/Oversized sunglasses/Cheerleader-esque ponytail/Seen reading

I do not (allegedly) kick cats like their neighbor Marge.

So they made me their queen.

Monologues were given about how my teeth were whiter than the teeth of their smoker mothers. Cartwheels and round-offs and flips were done in a circle around me. Tiny bodies attempted to breakdance. A seven year old in a pink bathrobe chased me, shouting out questions like a paparazzo.

They begged me never to move. Pleaded for me not to go inside, but stood in stunned excitement when I remembered all of their names as I said goodbye.

SMELLS LIKE BAD DECISIONS

It's like she's in a play that no one around her is acting in. Heavily scented. She's a pale pink and glossy black candy cane.

*

Dwindling to underweight and pressing your breasts together. Thigh highs and headbands. He'll be nice at first. All those years older than you rushing over you like waves. A martini and roofie sea. You salute your captain.

*

When you smell her perfume in the hall, you want to tell her no. *Whatever you're doing, no.*

*

She is too earnest, too serious to be in the circus. She thinks nothing of her little outfits, the show that will close. She's cupcake frosting, but thinks of herself as an instructional pamphlet.

THEY ARE DRINKING BOURBON AND I'M SURE THEY HAVE BEEN AT THIS TABLE SINCE THE 90S.

Sometimes when I am on a mediocre first date, I fantasize that the nearby table of boisterous women will adopt me. When they see my dark eyes melt into sad globs, they will carry me away from this man who considers New Kids on the Block a real band. *It's okay to cry*, they'll say, and place a paper crown on my head. I'll think about how much I love My Little Ponies and then get wasted.

INADEQUACY

My favorite thing about my job
is the tampons. Free tampons
in the bathroom, that is.
I am not paid in tampons.

I have the emotional health
of someone who is paid in
tampons. Tampons and stamps.

When people cover me with
stamps, I don't ask why.
I always assume I am meant
as a present for some important
person. I never think
Is this a prank?

REBIRTH

A twelve year old girl
runs barefoot in the woods
to escape her abductor.
Thorns from rose bushes
pierce her feet and legs.
She runs through a field,
a cemetery, crawls under
barbed wire. She whimpers
like a small animal,
getting the attention of farmers
who call 911. This sounds
like fiction, but it's a summary
from the news. The thorns
and the wrist still bound
by a zip tie, real. Bloodied,
the girl gives information.
There is still another girl
missing. A girl who didn't
sprint past the rural cemetery,
her own resurrection,
her body decorated with thorns.

EX'S EXIT

Boom bang bang goes the gun
I shoot. It sounds like the intro
of a pop song. I touch the trigger
lightly. There is no backfire.

I didn't want to kill him over
and over again. I never thought
this would be my reoccurring
fantasy. I didn't think it would
feel sexy and clean like
underwear with ruffles. I didn't know

my mind would become a neon
death scene. He fervently told me
about little girls. Most intense
desire, dream unapologetic.

I was already in my mid-twenties
when I first met him, but…
Is that your dad? my co-worker asked.
Pale purple tulips he gave me. Walks
we took in the summer dark.

It all faded, the flashbacks forming
pictures of nipples on flat chests
under tank tops, hazy portraits
of my own image, kneeling in prayer.
Bang bang boom goes the gun.

THE HAUNTING

1

So many nightmares I am relieved to wake from.

Missing too many college classes/I graduated years ago.

Being on stage not knowing the choreography/Never happened in real life; I'm no longer a professional dancer.

Purse stolen/Have purse.

Abducted/At home.

Math/No math.

But the other dreams.

My forty-something ex-boyfriend embracing a girl no older than twelve in the back of a car/This probably never happened … Probably won't happen … I tell myself after I am woken up by my own thrashing. He's savvy. Has a good job. He wouldn't. Or would never… let himself get caught.

Some people gamble. Some race cars. Flirtation with the boundary of…

My ex hung out with a sixteen-year-old girl. A so-called friend. Her parents knew him. He received photos from another friend, a gay fifty-something. In the photos, the man posed as a baby. Diaper, pacifier. Ex feigned disinterest, but his late night confessions, sexual attraction to the very young, floated in the air around my aching body.

Professor Perversion. Former love. My living ghost.

2

The second time my sixth grade teacher called me sounding drunk, my father said, *She's in bed. She's twelve.*

Oh, right. Sorry, man, said my sixth grade teacher to my father as if he was calling a grown woman and her boyfriend had picked up.

Upstairs, I was asleep, not dreaming of the first time he had called. Slurring his words and saying he had been thinking of me.

SEAS'N'S GREETINGS

How about we… shake our hips until my skirt swishes to pieces.

How about we… draw pictures of each other's hipbones.

How about we… start a publication called *Dutch Farmer Magazine*.

How about we… never speak to each other again when this doesn't go well.

How about we… blame all of our problems on each other in therapy.

How about we… fuck this shit.

Let's set each other on fire, then take pictures of our burns. Send postcards to friends and family featuring the burn photos. Greetings from two exes. Best wishes from our wounds.

AFTER FAKING MY DEATH

I burned my clothes
and my childhood toys.
My mother cried.
My father said the fire
wasn't necessary.

THEIR ORDEAL

It sounds like mac
and cheese. It sounds
like parents dating.
It sounds like a thirteen-
year-old girl traveling
to Dairy Queen
on a riding lawn mower
when no one will take her.
It sounds like a court date,
insomnia, dogs. When
a shoe breaks. Force
a smile. You love
everyone,
everyone.

FATHER °F THE BRIDE

Ingénues stolen in plain
sight. Girls, young women
assaulted on sunny days.

Your dad's car will not
be abandoned by a hiking trail.

Who wants to steal a father?
A tux fitting is not masculine.

Abandoned car pointed
in the wrong direction.
The father-daughter dance.
We may never know
what song he picked out.

DATEBOOK (SEPTEMBER-OCTOBER)

Package (no sender) waits for me.

—

Show me what a rampage is.

—

Seducing crazy sports announcer, bad idea.

—

Mail from ex. Howl at moon.

—

French fries, wine, ransom note.

—

Wear all my dresses backward now.

—

Established string quartet faces jail time.

—

Lemonade Stand, Ice Cream Truck Consolidation.

—

Can't be incognito with dresses backward.

—

Ghosts reorganize local youth football league.

KIRO, I KNOW YOUR REAL NAME

It's Bill. I know years before you ever
mentioned Butoh in interviews, you sold
your grandparents' furniture
on your San Francisco lawn until
everything got carried away.
I watch you now from the wings.
Your chalk white face and a silent
open mouth. You ran to the restroom
immediately after a meal. *I know
that ballerina dash*, said Robert.
I noticed a dozen or so men in uniform
out the restaurant's window and suddenly,
you were back faster than a zipper
can be pulled down and back up. After
making us watch you rehearse your solo
again, you cried that we are all
born alone and all die alone. *Duh.
You're just realizing this now?* I thought
as I nodded an exaggerated nod.

UNCANNY

1
Some of it's a haze.
Some of it I remember.
Wearing a green wig
in restaurants, squeezing
in multiple dates a day.
Nowhere near above average
promiscuous, but there's
no way I could remember
all the people I've kissed.
I could go without sleep
naturally for so long,
it made party-girl friends
worry about me.

2
My current co-workers joke
I'm in the CIA. Mysterious
because I'm never around.
I just can't get writing done
in an office with people
staring at me. They should
have known me then.
They would have fainted
from the amount of perfume
I was wearing. Felt
their hearts beat faster
hearing the click of my heels
in the hall. I would say
they would have talked
about me all day, like
I suspect they do now.

S° MUCH I WANT

I tried to move the bed
with my mind. I wanted
to lift it off the floor.
Smoothly. I wanted it
to rock back and forth
gently. Like a swing.
I could only get it
a few feet off the floor
before it came crashing
down with me on it.
Ouch. I tried to give
myself an orgasm
without touching myself,
taunted by something
I read in a magazine.
*Some women can reach
orgasm with only their minds.*
I got a headache from thinking
so hard and went back
to my finger-to-clit method.
My life isn't so bad.

PETITE SMACKS

You thought
I would write
a poem
for you
about
a girl
and a popsicle.
How slowly
she licks
it.

You thought
I would write
a poem
for you
about
men who stick
their mustaches
into place
with hairspray.
The Aqua Net,
the shame.

You asked
me why
my performance
art didn't
include
Snuffleupagus
and a reenactment
of your birth.

You asked
me why
when I see you
I look
away
and kick
rocks.

EXTENDED

A female deer is generally alone through
most of the year.

Take a needle and thread through
dough, some soil, a body of water.

It's the horror of discovering who/what
you are really in love with. Performer

= Introvert = Peril / I pray
for health, but fantasize about amnesia.

I tell acquaintances, dates
anytime from the other side

of the door.

ACKNOWLEDGMENTS

Thank you to the following publications, where poems from this manuscript originally appeared:

The Alarmist Magazine
Alba: A Journal of Short Poetry
Anthem Journal
Barely South Review
Cease, Cows
Chiron Review
Eleven Eleven
Hobart
Lemon Hound
Nashville Review
The Orange Room Review
Painted Bride Quarterly
Ping-Pong: Journal of Henry Miller Library
The Puritan
San Pedro River Review
Squalorly
Sugar House Review
Superstition Review
Verdad

Vine Leaves Literary Journal

WHAT WE WANT

The written vignette:

"Vignette" is a word that originally meant "something that may be written on a vine leaf." It's a snapshot in words. It differs from flash fiction or a short story in that its aim does not lie within the realms of traditional structure or plot. The vignette focuses on one element, mood, character, setting or object. It's descriptive, excellent for character or theme exploration and wordplay. Through a vignette, you create an atmosphere.

A vignette can be written in a variety of forms.

We're looking for:

prose   poetry   script

We will accept all genres except erotica. Write something brilliant and woo us into publishing it!

The visual vignette:

Artwork or photography will be considered for the cover and interior of each issue. Send us a piece of work you believe represents a slice of life.

WHEN TO SUBMIT

Submissions are open all year round.
We publish biannually online and in print.

To be published in our MAY ISSUE, submit between September 1st – February 28th.

To be published in our NOVEMBER ISSUE, submit between March 1st – August 31st.

Visit our website for further guidelines:
vineleavesliteraryjournal.com

PAYMENT

We pay $5 AUD per acceptance into the journal. This means if we accept 1 poem, you'll get $5. If we accept three pieces of prose, you'll get $5. If we accept two poems and three prose and one photo, you'll get $5. At the moment we can only issue payment via PayPal. OR, you can receive a contributor copy of the print journal instead of payment.

Vine Leaves Literary Journal — © 2011—2015
Australia & Greece
Online ISSN: 2202-2767 — Print ISSN: 2204-4574
Vine Leaves Press — Australia & Greece
ABN: 39159817423
All staff are volunteers.
vineleaves.editors@gmail.com

The Annual Vine Leaves Vignette Collection Award

Submissions open: June 1 – February 28.

Includes a cash prize of $500 (USD), publication by Vine Leaves Press (paperback and eBook), 20 copies of the paperback, worldwide distribution, and promotion through *Vine Leaves Literary Journal* and staff websites. Author will receive a 70% net royalty on all eBook and print sales.

Visit *vineleavesliteraryjournal.com/vine-leaves-vignette -collection-award* for details.

Please visit *vineleavesliteraryjournal.com* for submission guidelines.

www.vineleavesliteraryjournal.com/donate

Vine Leaves Literary Journal now tallies more than 4000 unique views a month and the compliments we've been receiving by email make this job worth every second of effort.

This is thanks to YOU. Without your brilliant poetry, prose and art, this journal would not exist.

But the more we grow, the more we start to scrape the bottom of the money barrel. Especially since we are now publishing full-length books through Vine Leaves Press in both paperback and eBook. But this means any money that we receive goes straight back into the journal and paying contributors for their work.

Our piggy bank is always on the brink of empty. We have tried to acquire grant support through the Australian Council for the Arts, but in order to be eligible, we have to publish only Australian literature.

We are not willing to do that. There is a *world* of amazing writers out there!

Can you help us?

Please do us the honour of donating a few bucks to our mission: to give the vignette, a forgotten literary form, the exposure and credit it deserves.

Just think of it as buying two coffees one morning, instead of one, for the greater good of the vignette!

Thanks,
The Vine Leaves Team

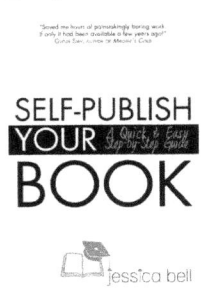

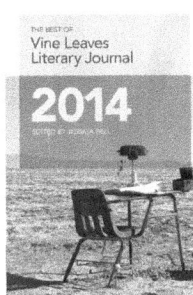

Vine Leaves Literary Journal was founded to offer the vignette, a forgotten literary form, the exposure and credit it deserves.

The journal, published quarterly online, is a lush synergy of atmospheric prose, poetry, photography and illustrations, put together with an eye for aesthetics as well as literary merit. The annual print anthology showcases the very best pieces from throughout the year.

Each vignette merges to create a vivid snapshot in time and place. Prepare for big stories in small spaces, between and beyond the words.

Read one at a time.

Taste them. Savour them.

Live them.

www.vineleavesliteraryjournal.com

www.ingramcontent.com/pod-product-compliance
Lightning Source LLC
Chambersburg PA
CBHW070928280326
41934CB00009B/1785